Quiz

12652

PTS
2.0

FRANCIS PARKMAN AND THE

PLAINS INDIANS

**HISTORY
EYEWITNESS**

EDITED WITH AN INTRODUCTION
AND ADDITIONAL MATERIAL BY
JANE SHUTER

RSVP

**RAINTREE
STECK-VAUGHN**
PUBLISHERS
The Steck-Vaughn Company

Austin, Texas

Published by Raintree Steck-Vaughn Publishers, an imprint of Steck-Vaughn Company

Design by Saffron House, map by Jeff Edwards.

Library of Congress Cataloging-in-Publication Data
Francis Parkman and the Plains Indians / edited with an
    introduction and additional material by Jane Shuter.
        p.   cm. — (History eyewitness)
    Includes index.
    ISBN 0-8114-8280-4
    1. Parkman, Francis, 1823-1893 — Juvenile literature.
2. Indianists — Great Plains —Biography — Juvenile literature.
3. Indians of North America — Great Plains — History —
Juvenile literature.   4. Indians of North America — Great
Plains — Social life and customs — Juvenile literature.
I. Shuter, Jane.   II. Title.   III. Series.
E76.45.P37F73   1995
978'.00497'0092—dc20   94-12853
[B]   CIP   AC

Printed in China
Bound in the United States

1 2 3 4 5 6 7 8 9 0 LB 99 98 97 96 95 94

Acknowledgments
The publishers would like to thank the following for permission to reproduce photographs:

American Museum of Natural History, N. Y.: p.35 *top*
    (J. Beckett, D. Finnin)
Beinecke Rare Book and Manuscript Library/Yale University:
    pp.8-9
Buffalo Bill Historical Center, Cody, Wyoming/Gift of the
    Coe Foundation: p.6
Chip Clark/National Museum of Natural History/Smithsonian
    Institution: p.15
Gilcrease Museum, Tulsa: p.12
Joslyn Art Museum, Omaha, Nebraska: pp.21, 22 (and cover)
    43, 44-45
National Museum of American Art, Washington, D.C./Art
    Resource, N.Y.: pp.19, 40-41
National Museum of American Art, Washington, D.C. Gift of
    Mrs. Joseph Harrison, Jr.: pp.11, 26-27, 29
Peter Newark's Western Americana: pp. 24, 32-33, 39
Pitt Rivers Museum, Oxford/Philip Parkhouse: pp.35
    below, 36
The Saint Louis Art Museum, Gift of Mrs. John T. Davis: p.1

The photograph on pp.30-31 is reprinted from A Pictographic
History of the Oglala Sioux by Amos Bad Heart Bull, text by
Helen H. Glish, by permission of the University of Nebraska
Press. Copyright © 1967 by the University of Nebraska Press

Every effort has been made to contact copyright holders of material reproduced in this book. Any omissions will be rectified in subsequent printings if notice is given to the publisher.

Note to the Reader

In this book some of the words are printed in **bold** type. This indicates that the word is listed in the glossary on pages 46-47. The glossary gives a brief explanation of words that may be new to you.

CONTENTS

Introduction

Francis Parkman came from a rich family. He lived in Boston, went to private school, and then on to Harvard University in 1840. Parkman was enthusiastic about many things. His enthusiasms at Harvard included acting and chemistry, but even then he was described as having "Indians on the brain." He spent his vacations going on "wilderness" excursions and in learning to shoot. In 1843 he spent some months visiting Europe, then returned and took his degree from Harvard in 1844. Parkman then went to Law School; he never intended to practice law, but, he said, went "for the mental training that it offered the brain."

In April 1846, when Parkman was 23, he and Quincy Adams Shaw set off on their journey along the Oregon Trail. The aim was to satisfy Parkman's curiosity about the Native Americans, to help his health, and to give him the material to write a book. It did not help his health. When he returned to Boston in October 1846, his health broke down completely. The book on which this story is based was dictated to his cousin and was published first as a series of articles, then as a book. It was titled *The Oregon Trail*.

Parkman's illness was a weakness of the nervous system and meant he often spent many months unable to get out of bed. One French doctor even predicted that he might one day go mad, although this did not happen. He was not a miserable person, despite his constant illness, and was determined to go on working, fixing up special reading and writing devices for his bedroom. Despite sometimes writing no more than six lines a day, Parkman went on to write several books on American history. He married Catherine Scolley, the daughter of a Boston doctor, in 1850. They had two daughters and then a son, who died. Catherine died within a year of the boy. Parkman sent his daughters to live with their aunt and went to live with his parents. He said it took him at least four years to recover from the shock of the two deaths. He died after an attack of peritonitis on November 8, 1893.

It was quite common for wealthy people to go off to explore "the frontier" at this time. They would hire the equipment and animals they needed, and also guides and other people to work for them, such as muleteers to manage the animals. This was a time when many Native Americans were still welcoming to strangers – although there were some who had never been friendly, either to white men or to people from any other tribe. Things were changing, though, and Parkman predicted in his book, with some accuracy, the breakdown of friendly relations between Indians and whites.

Parkman's route followed the Oregon Trail for a long way. This was one of the main routes taken by settlers.

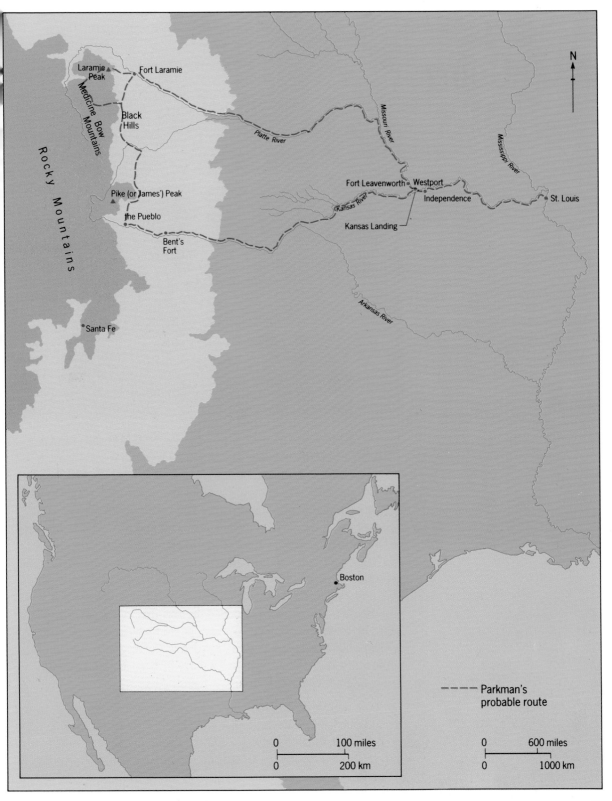

N

Laramie
Peak
Fort Laramie

Medicine Bow Mountains

Black
Hills

Rocky Mountains

Platte River

Missouri River

Mississippi River

Pike (or James') Peak

Fort Leavenworth • Westport
Independence

St. Louis

Kansas River

the Pueblo

Kansas Landing

Bent's
Fort

Arkansas River

Santa Fe

Boston

0   100 miles

0   200 km

— — — Parkman's
probable route

0   600 miles

0   1000 km

5

CHAPTER I

Going West

Traveling to "the West" was a gentleman's pastime at this time. Some of the more well-off gentlemen even had artists traveling with them to record the journey. This picture was painted by Alfred Jacob Miller, who traveled the West with Sir William Drummond Stewart in 1837. It shows the Indians firing their rifles in greetings.

My friend Quincy Adams Shaw and myself left St. Louis on April 28, 1846, on a tour of curiosity and amusement in the Rocky Mountains. We traveled on a **steamboat**, the *Radnor*, which was heavily loaded. On her upper decks were large wagons crammed with goods to trade in Santa Fe, and her holds were crammed with goods for the same destination. There were also the equipment and provisions of a party of Oregon **emigrants**, a band of mules and horses, piles of saddles and harnesses, and a multitude of other articles indispensable on the **prairies**. Almost hidden in this medley was our small French cart, a tent, and a miscellaneous assortment of boxes and barrels. The passengers on the *Radnor* matched the **freight**. In her cabin were Santa Fe traders, gamblers, speculators, and adventurers of various descriptions. Her steerage was crowded with Oregon emigrants, **"mountain men," Negroes**, and a party of Kansas Indians, who had been on a visit to St. Louis.

The boat struggled for eight days up the Missouri, against the current, catching its keel on the bottom, and hanging for two to three hours at a time on the shifting sandbars that are a feature of the river. The river shifts continually, and the islands on it regularly collapse, leaving exposed branches and trunks of trees as a further hazard.

We noticed parties of emigrants all along the banks, making their way to the rendezvous at Independence. We left the boat at Kansas, about 500 miles from the mouth of the Missouri. We then took a wagon to Westport to get horses, mules, and guides for the journey. Westport was full of Indians, whose shaggy little ponies were tied up by the dozen along the houses and fences. **Sacs** and **Foxes**, with shaved heads and painted faces, **Shawanoes** [Shawnees] and **Delawares**, fluttering in calico frocks and turbans, **Wyandots** dressed like white men, and a few wretched **Kansas** wrapped in old blankets were strolling about the streets, or lounging in and out of the shops and houses.

We met a British army captain and his brother, whom we recognized from the steamer, and arranged to travel with them. They were already installed in Westport, and had hired mules and a guide. They were staying in a little log house, where they had collected all the **appointments** necessary for the prairie. The Captain, who had a taste for natural history, was engaged in stuffing a woodpecker. They were much more ready for the journey than we were, and eventually went on ahead, arranging to meet us at the crossing of the Kansas River. We hired ourselves a scout called Deslauriers. We then received a message saying that they had gone on further, making a change of route that they had not consulted us about, and would meet up with us at Fort Leavenworth. We considered the change of plan somewhat high-handed, but decided to join them anyhow. We set off, but our first step was an unfortunate one. One of the mules was no sooner put between the shafts than she reared and plunged and nearly flung the whole cart into the Missouri. We finally traded her for another mule, but Westport was scarcely out of sight when we encountered a deep muddy ditch, one of a sort that was to become all too familiar to us, and here for the space of an hour or two we stuck fast. Eventually we started out on our journey.

TRAVELING COMPANIONS

It was the custom for white people on the frontier to travel in fairly large groups, for this way they were less likely to be attacked or come to grief in any natural disasters. Parkman's traveling companions changed several times, depending on chance meetings and emergencies.

CHAPTER 2

Fort Laramie

After many adventures, and some wearisome time spent traveling with a band of emigrants, we finally reached Fort Laramie. It was at Fort Laramie that we first met with the Dakota Indians. The Dakota range over a vast territory, from the St. Peter River to the Rocky Mountains. They have several independent bands, but have the same language and beliefs. Each band is divided into villages, each with a chief. Chiefs have power in proportion to the fear and respect they inspire, and may lose this power at any time. The Western Dakota have no fixed habitation. They wander incessantly, hunting and fighting. They follow the buffalo, which provide them with the necessities of life: homes, food, clothing, bedding, fuel, string for their bows, glue, thread, ropes for the horses, coverings for their saddles, containers for food and water, boats to cross streams, and the means of trade with white men. When the buffalo are extinct, the Dakota too must dwindle away.

Having lived among them, I could observe them. They were wild. Neither their manners nor their ideas were in the slightest degree modified by contact with **civilization**. Their religion, superstitions, and prejudices were those handed down to them from time immemorial. They fought with the weapons that their fathers used and wore the same garments of skins. They were living representations of the "stone age"; for though their lances and arrows were tipped with metal procured from the traders, they still used the crude stone **mallets** of the **primeval** world.

PIPE SMOKING

Native American men smoked their pipes for several different reasons. Mainly they smoked to be sociable, as part of the evening's activities. They would also smoke, however, as part of religious rituals, and as part of peace-making. On these occasions only certain people were allowed to join in.

Fort Laramie, painted by Alfred Jacob Miller in 1837. The fort was not, at this time, a fort set up by soldiers to fight the Indians. It was a place to trade, and Native American tribes used to camp regularly on the plains nearby.

Fort Laramie is one of the trading posts established by the "American Fur Company," which monopolizes the Indian trade of the region. Its officials rule absolutely; the army has little force. Most evenings Shaw and I visited the Dakota camp of chief Old Smoke nearby, for Shaw would act as doctor for any minor ills. Old Smoke's **lodge** was no better than the others, indeed it was rather shabby. In this **democratic** community the chief never assumes a superior state. Smoke sat cross-legged on a **buffalo robe** and watched Shaw treat the patients, most of them women and children, and most of them with **inflammations** of the eyes, caused by exposure to the sun. He treated these ailments with **homeopathic** cures, and was the first to do so among the Oglala Sioux.

During the treatment, Old Smoke's oldest **squaw** entered with a stone mallet in her hand and took a puppy from the litter that was huddled in one corner of the lodge. She carried it to the entrance of the lodge and killed it. She then swung the carcass to and fro over a fire to singe off the hair. This done she chopped it into small pieces, dropped it into a **kettle** of hot water, and in a few moments we were offered a large wooden dish of dog meat. This was the greatest compliment a Dakota could pay, so we forced ourselves to eat, though we had to do so under the gaze of the puppy's unknowing parent. Meanwhile Old Smoke was preparing his great pipe. When we had eaten, he lit the pipe, and we passed it back and forth until the pipe was empty. After this we left and returned to the fort.

LODGES

Parkman called the homes of the Indians lodges. They were also called "tepees." They were tents made from buffalo hides stretched around wooden poles, in a circular shape, with a hole at the top for the smoke to escape through. Although Parkman found them very dark and cramped, they were ideal homes for people who were constantly on the move. The poles could be used to form a sort of stretcher, called a "travois," to carry their belongings when they moved on, and the hides that formed the walls were light and fairly easily folded.

CHAPTER 3

Indian Wars

In the summer of 1846, there was much fighting between the Dakotas and the Snake tribes. This caused much coming and going and rumors in the fort. We were told that many Indians, five or six thousand, were heading for La Bonté's Camp, where they would celebrate their war ceremonies, and then set out to fight the Snake tribe. I was glad to hear this, for I wanted to study the Indians close at hand, and was keen to see their war ceremonies. I also hoped, by going to La Bonté's Camp, to attach myself to a particular village so that I could travel with them and observe their ways. We resolved to go to the meeting at La Bonté's Camp ourselves.

One morning, coming out from breakfast with a trader named McCluskey, I saw a strange Dakota by the gate to the fort, a tall strong man with heavy features. I asked who he was. "That's The Whirlwind," said McCluskey. "He is at the bottom of all this fighting. The Sioux are like this; they never stop cutting each other's throats. If this war goes on, we'll have a poor trade with them next year; they won't have time to make the buffalo robes ready for us."

McCluskey said that there were already six villages gathered together some forty miles distant, calling to the **Great Spirit** to help them. We were hoping to travel to La Bonté's Camp in the company of Reynal, a vagrant Indian trader. We were worried about our safety on the journey, but met with no trouble. After some days we met a Dakota called Mahto-Tatonka, or Bull Bear, and three other warriors. We shook hands and gave them coffee and biscuits, at which they exclaimed "How! How!" from the bottom of their throats. This word is used almost all the time by the Indians to convey a variety of feelings. Bull Bear said his village was two days to the south of us, and that they too would go to war. We traveled on with them, but when we reached the place chosen as the last camping ground before La Bonté's Camp, it was empty. Bull Bear's village was not there. We pitched our tent and rode to find them. All we found was a single Native American who said that they would be at least three days late joining us.

A day passed, and Indians began rapidly to come in. Parties of two or three would ride up and silently seat themselves on the grass. On the fourth day the main party came, a wild procession, hurrying toward us in great disorder. There were horses, mules, and dogs, heavily burdened **travois,** warriors on horseback, squaws on foot, and a host of children. For a full half hour, they poured into the camp ground, following the bend in the stream. They seemed nothing but a dark confused throng; then, as if by magic, one hundred fifty tall lodges sprang up. The lonely plain was transformed into the site of a swarming encampment. Countless horses were soon grazing on the prairie, and then we caught sight of a familiar white-robed figure. The Whirlwind had come at last.

NATIVE AMERICAN MEETING PLACES

The Sioux were nomads; they traveled the plains following the buffalo. Each tribe moved inside certain recognized areas. There were also certain places that were recognized as meeting places for several tribes at particular times. La Bonté's Camp was probably one of these.

This picture of a Dakota chief called Smoke was painted by George Catlin in 1832. This chief may have been the chief that Parkman met. He could have been called "old" when Parkman was in the area in 1847 and is a chief of the right tribe, living in the right area. On the other hand, many Indians would have had this name, so we cannot be certain.

While we were waiting for the village to decide what to do, I was stricken by an illness that had been gaining on me since Fort Laramie. It was a weakness that meant I could hardly stand, and I walked like a drunken man. Things often seemed to sway before my eyes, and scenes of camp life passed before me as in a dream.

At last The Whirlwind and his warriors decided to move on. Despite their many nights of preparation for war, with ceremonies and dancing, they had decided not to go to La Bonté's Camp, but to go to hunt buffalo on the other side of the Black Hills, at least until they had enough hides to make new lodges. After this they might send out a small war party, which might, or might not, join any others. This put us in a difficult position. Should we stay with them, or try to reach La Bonté's Camp? Those villages might also decide against a war party. We were coming to realize that Indians were much given to

An Indian Council, painted by Seth Eastman in 1852. Decisions in Indian villages were made by the chief and the oldest and most important warriors. They would meet together, sit in a circle, and share a pipe of tobacco until either agreement was reached, or the village split up for a while, possibly meeting again later.

changing their minds. There might even be no Indians at the Camp at all. Reynal said we should go with The Whirlwind, as it was most unlikely that there would be any Indians at the Camp. Recalling the old proverb about "a bird in the hand," we decided to stay with The Whirlwind's village.

We broke camp on July 1. We had been traveling for half a day when we met some white traders who assured us that there was a gathering of ten or twelve villages that intended to go to war but a day's march away. Shaw and I decided to join these Indians, but traveled with our present Indian friends as far as the night's camp, for our paths lay in the same direction. That night in camp it was clear that the younger warriors were still set on war, for they galloped in circles around the camp, each singing his war song. Some of the clothes were superb. They had crests of feathers, and tunics of antelope skins that fit them closely. Their tunics were fringed with the scalps of their enemies; their shields fluttered with eagle feathers. All had bows and arrows on their backs, and a few had lances or guns. As each noted champion warrior passed, the old women cried out their names to honor their bravery. In the morning the Indians set off westward, and we headed north to look for the war-gathering that we had been told about.

When we reached the place he had mentioned, we saw, not a plain covered with encampments and swarming with life, but a vast unbroken desert without any bush, tree, or sign of life. Overcome by the futility of it all, I gave in to my sickness in full earnest. The others went out in search of the Indians, but found none. It was decided, after some days, to split up, meeting back at Fort Laramie on August 1. Raymond and I set out to try to trace the Whirlwind's village, while Shaw and Deslauriers went back to Fort Laramie with the cart and most of the baggage. Raymond and I set off with his mule and my horse heavily laden. We blundered about on the prairie for many days, when at last from the top of a hill we saw buffalo, a stream, and beside the stream, an Indian village.

GOING TO WAR

The tribes of the Sioux often fought among themselves. They were proud people, and if they felt they had been insulted, they would often resort to fighting to settle the matter. On the other hand, war was not, as it was to the whites, a matter of assembling huge armies and weapons, giving a formal declaration of war and fighting set battles and skirmishes until there was either a definite winner or a peace was made. War could be agreed on and then never actually be fought, depending on how many people came to the gathering and whether there was anything of more importance that had come up while the villages were traveling to the meeting place. Parkman could not understand the way the Indians seemed to be forever changing their minds. As far as the Indians were concerned, the war they were discussing was important, but in the end it was not as important as making sure that they had homes for the next winter.

BUFFALO HUNTING

Reynal talks of making a surround. This was one method of hunting which consisted of literally surrounding a buffalo and killing it. Methods of killing and hunting varied, depending on the number of Indians in the band, what weapons they had, how many buffalo they needed to kill, and if they had horses or not. There is evidence that prehistoric Indians killed enough animals to stay alive by driving them over cliffs. Later they would creep up on the buffalo in bands, and then try to kill them with stone-tipped lances and arrows. Once they had horses and rifles, they would often stampede the buffalo, and then each Indian would chase an animal.

A Dakota lodge, bought by the Smithsonian Museum in 1874. This shows how the lodge was fitted together. The flaps at the top can be fixed onto the poles to keep the wind from blowing the smoke back into the lodge. The bottom flaps of the lodge could be raised in the summer to allow a draft to circulate, while in the winter they were dropped down to keep in the warmth.

As soon as Raymond and I saw the village from the gap in the hills, we were also seen; keen eyes were constantly on the watch. As we rode down upon the plain, the side of the village nearest to us was darkened with a crowd of naked figures. Several men came forward to meet us. I could distinguish among them the green blanket of Reynal. When we came up, the ceremony of shaking hands had to be gone through in due form, and then all were eager to know what had become of the rest of my party. I told them, and then we moved toward the village. "You've missed it," said Reynal. "If you'd been here the day before yesterday, you'd have found the whole prairie over yonder black with buffalo as far as you could see. There were no cows though, nothing but bulls. We made a **surround** every day until yesterday. See the village there; don't that look like good living?"

I could see, even at that distance, long cords stretched from lodge to lodge, over which the meat, cut by the squaws into thin sheets, was hanging to dry in the sun. I noticed, too, that the village was smaller than when I had last seen it, and asked Reynal why. He said that old Le Bogne had felt too weak to cross the mountains and had stayed behind with his relations, including Mahto-Tatonka and all his brothers. The Whirlwind, too, had been unwilling to come so far, Reynal said, because he was afraid. Only half a dozen lodges had stayed with him; most of the village had set their chief's authority at naught, and taken the course most agreeable to their inclinations. Reynal suggested that we stay with Big Crow, as he was known to favor white men. So, still followed by a crowd of Indians, Raymond and I rode up to the entrance of Big Crow's lodge. A squaw came out immediately and took our horses. I put aside the leather flap that covered the low opening and, stooping, entered Big Crow's dwelling. There I could see the chief in the dim light, seated to one side on a pile of buffalo robes. He greeted me with a guttural "How, cola!" and I asked Reynal to tell him that Raymond and I were come to live with him. This may seem intrusive, but every Indian in the village would have felt honored that white men should choose his hospitality.

The squaw spread a buffalo robe for us in the guest's place in the lodge. Our saddles were brought in, and scarcely were we seated upon them, before the place was thronging with Native Americans, crowding in to see us. Big Crow produced his pipe and filled it with a mixture of tobacco and red willow bark. Round and round it passed, and a lively conversation took place. Meanwhile a squaw placed before the two guests a wooden bowl of boiled buffalo meat. This was not the only banquet to be inflicted on us. One after another, boys and young squaws thrust their heads in at the opening to invite us to feasts in different parts of the village.

14

This is a buffalo dance, painted by Charles Wimar in the 1830s. Native Americans believed that they could use ritual dances to affect both the nature and behavior of the animals. The buffalo dance was supposed to ensure a good hunt.

For half an hour or more, we passed from lodge to lodge, tasting in each the bowl of meat set before us, and inhaling a whiff or two from our host's pipe. A thunderstorm, which had been threatening for some time now, began in good earnest. We crossed over to Reynal's lodge, though it hardly deserved the name, for it consisted only of a few old buffalo robes supported on poles, and was quite open on one side. While the thunderstorm raged around us, we discussed Indian beliefs about what caused the thunder, and this caused much debate, and what seemed to be actual disagreement among the Indians. Finally Mene-Seela, or Red Water, said that the thunder was a great black bird.

He had seen it once, he said, in a dream, swooping down from the Black Hills with loud roaring wings, striking lightning out of the lakes as it passed. Another Indian announced that the thunder had killed his brother the previous summer. The dead man had belonged to a group of Indians who claimed the right and privilege of fighting the thunder as part of their lodge's magic powers. When a storm threatened, the thunder fighters would take their bows and arrows, their magic drum, and a sort of whistle made out of the wing bone of a war eagle, and, thus equipped, run out and fire at the thunder cloud, whooping, yelling, whistling, and beating the drum to frighten it away. The dead man had been killed during this ceremony by a lightning bolt striking the point of his lance.

Big Crow's lodge presented a picturesque spectacle that evening. A score or more of Indians were sitting in a circle, just visible by the dull light of the fire in the middle. The pipe glowed brightly in the gloom as it passed from hand to hand. From time to time a squaw would drop a piece of buffalo fat onto the fire, and a bright flame would leap up, darting light to the very top of the lodge. The light gilded the features of the Indians as they sat around it, telling their endless stories of war and hunting. It also lit the skin garments hung around the lodge, the bow, **quiver**, and lance hung over the place of the chief, and our own rifles and powder horns. For a moment all would be bright as day, then the light would fade, and all would be obscure again.

MAGIC AND LODGES

The Indians believed in magic, and believed that they could influence nature by performing particular ceremonies, like the buffalo dance shown on this page. Although the Indians traveled in village groups, many of the men were also organized into lodges, religious groups that had members in many of the villages. So the word *lodge* had two meanings, the family home, or a particular religious group. Some lodges performed ceremonies to affect the behavior of animals; others tried to affect nature, like the thunder fighters. Others performed magic that was supposed to weaken the enemy in battle.

Parkman's Feast

As I left the lodge next morning, most of the dogs in the village rushed to attack me. They were as cowardly as they were noisy, and kept their distance; only one little cur had spirit enough to make a direct attack. He dashed at the tassel of my **moccasin,** which in Dakota fashion, was trailing on the ground behind me. He took hold and held on, growling, although every step I made nearly bowled him over. I knew the whole village was watching to see if I showed signs of fear, so I walked on, without looking right or left, surrounded by this circle of dogs. When I reached Reynal's lodge, I sat down outside it, and the dogs dispersed. Only one large white one remained, running before me and showing his teeth. He was fat and sleek, just the dog I wanted. "My friend," I thought, "you shall pay for this! I will have you eaten this very morning."

I intended to give the Indians a feast to show I had good character and dignity. A white dog is a dish that the Dakota customarily eat at all occasions of formality and importance. I consulted Reynal, who said the dog belonged to the woman in the next lodge. I took a bright cotton handkerchief and laid it on the ground, arranging on it some **vermilion,** beads, and other **trinkets.** The squaw was called. I pointed to the dog and to the handkerchief. She gave a scream of delight, snatched up her prize, and vanished into the lodge. For a few more trifles, two other squaws killed the dog, singed his fur off on a fire, chopped him up, and put him into two kettles to boil. I had Raymond fry what flour we had in buffalo fat and make a kettle of tea. Big Crow's squaw swept out the lodge for the feast, and I asked my host to invite the guests, so as to miss no one I should honor.

For a feast one hour of the day serves the Indian as well as any other. Things were ready at eleven o' clock in the morning. Raymond and Reynal walked across the village carrying the two kettles of dog meat slung on a pole between them. These they placed in the center of the lodge. I had put on a pair of brilliant moccasins, and a coat I had brought for public occasions. I also made careful use of the razor, which should not be neglected if you wish to gain the good opinion of the Indians. Raymond, Reynal, and I then sat at the head of the lodge. The guests came in and sat on the ground, wedged in a close circle. Each had a wooden bowl to hold his share of the meal. When all were there, two

A Sioux dog feast, painted by George Catlin in the 1830s. It has been painted as if the circular lodge had been opened up, so that we can see what is going on. It would, in fact, have been much more cramped than this seems. This feast has finished, because the bowls are upside down by the pots, and pipe smoking has begun.

officials came forward with ladles made of the horns of the Rocky Mountain sheep and distributed the feast, giving a double share to the chiefs and the old men. Then each guest turned his dish upside down to show that all was gone. The bread was distributed, followed by the tea, all into the same bowls. I noticed that the tea had a strange color. "Oh," said Reynal, "there was not enough tea, so I stirred some soot into the kettle to make it look strong." Luckily the tea was well sweetened, and that was enough for the Indians.

The feasting was done, so the speech-making began. Pipes were filled, and I made my speech, which Reynal translated sentence by sentence as I went along. All through the speech the Indians greeted each sentence with cries of "How!" variously intonated to express agreement, wonder, or approval.

"I come from a far country where the white men are as numerous as blades of grass on the prairie, the squaws are more beautiful than you can imagine, and the men are all brave warriors. I had heard of the bravery of the Oglala Sioux, that they were a great nation, of their kindness to white men, and of their cleverness in the hunt and in **counting coup**. I decided to see if this was true for myself. Because I came on horseback through the mountains, I could not bring many presents for you, yet I have bought some tobacco and some powder, shot, and knives. I wish to give these now, and if you come to see me at Fort Laramie before I leave, I will be able to give you far more handsome presents."

Here Raymond and Reynal cut up and gave out the three or four pounds of tobacco that I had bought at Fort Laramie.

I was thanked in a long speech by Mene-Seela, the gist of which was that they had always loved the white man; whites were the wisest people on the earth. He was glad I had come, and the reason for not bringing more presents was plain. It was clear that I liked them, or I would not have made the long journey to meet them. Serious speeches over, we sat and chatted and smoked. Suddenly Mene-Seela broke in, saying in a loud voice:

"As all the chiefs are here, it would be a good time to decide what to do now. We came over the mountains to get hides to repair our lodges for next year, as the old ones are rotten and worn out. We have killed plenty of bull buffalos, but we have found no herds of cow buffalos, and the hides of bull buffalo are too thick and heavy for the squaws to make into lodges. There must be plenty of cows by the Medicine Bow Mountains. We should go there. I know it is further west than we have ever gone, and perhaps the Snake will attack us, for those hunting grounds are theirs. But our old lodges will not last another year. We should not fear the Snakes. Our warriors are brave; they are ready for

war. Besides, we have three white men and their rifles to help us."

There was a lot of talk, which I could not follow, and it seemed as though most agreed with this. Then Mene-Seela sang a discordant chant that we were told was a song of thanks for the feast, and the Indians left. For some time the chief walked about the village singing his song in praise of the feast, as is the custom of the nation.

As the day came to an end, the horses came in from the plains, to be **picketed** by the lodges of their masters. Soon within the great circle of lodges appeared another circle of restless horses, and here and there fires flickered in the gloom. I went to Reynal's lodge to ask if we would move on in the morning. Eagle-Feather, Mene-Seela's son, was there. He said that no one could know, for since the old chief died, the people were like children that did not know their own minds.

A painting by Karl Bodmer showing the burial scaffold of an Indian chief, 1837. Indians who were seen as important were buried in wooden scaffolds, out in the open, high enough up so that scavenging animals could not get to their bones.

21

Chapter 5

Moving On

A picture of a Dakota camp, painted by Karl Bodmer in 1833. The women did the work around the camp. They put the camp up and took it down again. They cooked the food and prepared the buffalo hides. They cared for the children and waited on the warriors at all times.

When I came up from my wash in the river the next morning, I saw that we were to move. Some of the lodges were already reduced to skeletons of poles as the squaws removed the hides and packed them. One or two respected chiefs, it seemed, had decided to move on and set their squaws to packing up, so the rest of the village was following their example. One by one the lodges were sinking down, and where the great circle of the village had been only moments before, nothing now remained but a ring of horses and Indians, crowded together in confusion. The ruins of the lodges were spread on the ground, with kettles, stone mallets, horn ladles, buffalo robes, and cases of painted hide filled with dried meat. Squaws bustled about in busy preparation, the old women screaming to each other at the full stretch of their leathern lungs. The shaggy ponies were patiently standing while the lodge poles were lashed to their sides, and the baggage piled on their backs. The dogs, with their tongues lolling out, lay lazily panting and waiting for the time of departure. Each warrior sat on the ground by the decaying embers of his fire, unmoved amid the confusion, holding in his hand the long trail rope of his horse.

As their preparations were completed, each family moved off the ground. The crowd was rapidly melting away. I could see them crossing the river and passing in quick succession along the line of the hill on the farther side. When all were gone, Raymond and I mounted

and set out after them, and as we gained the summit, the whole village came into view at once, straggling away for a mile or more over the barren plains. Everywhere glittered the iron points of lances. There were heavy laden pack horses, led by some wretched old woman, with two or three children clinging to their backs. There were mules and ponies covered from head to tail with gaudy trappings, ridden by some gay young squaw. Boys with miniature bows and arrows wandered over the plains, little naked children scampered about on foot, and numberless dogs darted in and out of the horses' feet. The young braves, gaudy with paint and feathers, rode in groups among the crowd, often galloping, two or three at once, along the line to test the speed of their horses. Here and there you might see a rank of sturdy pedestrians stalking along in their white buffalo robes. These were the **dignitaries** of the village, the old men and warriors to whose age and experience the people gave a silent deference. With the rough prairies and the broken hills for its background, the restless scene was striking and picturesque beyond description. Days and weeks made me familiar with it, but I never ceased to wonder at it.

As we moved on, the broken column grew yet more scattered and disorderly until, as we approached the foot of a hill, I saw the old men sit down in a row upon the ground, as if marking a line. They lit a pipe and sat smoking, laughing, and telling stories, while the people, stopping as they came up one after the other, also sat and were soon gathered in a crowd behind them. Soon everyone had caught up. Then the old men rose, pulled their buffalo robes around their shoulders, and went on as before. Now the ground was steep, and the descent of the hill was something to watch. There was not a minute's pause. The group descended in a mass, amid dust and confusion. The horses braced their hooves as they went down, slipping and throwing up dust, the women and children were screaming, and the dogs yelped as they were trodden on.

We camped late that afternoon, and my old illness came on me. I fell asleep and slept totally unconscious until the next morning. The first thing that woke me was a flapping sound over my head and a sudden light breaking in over me as Big Crow's squaws dismantled the lodge around me. I shook off my blanket with the feeling of perfect health,

CIRCLES

The circle was an important shape to the Native Americans; it had magical significance. Their lodges were circular, and their camps were put up, wherever possible, to form a circle around a central meeting ground. An Indian chief, Black Elk, said: "Everything an Indian does is a circle, and that is because the power of the world works in circles; even the seasons form a great circle, and come back to where they were before. Our tepees are round, like birds' nests, and they are set in a circle, the nation's hoop, a nest of many nests, where the Great Spirit meant us to raise our children."

An Indian woman preparing to move on. Everything the family owned would be carefully packed onto the travois, the sledge that the horse would pull. Notice the man sitting in the background. Indian men took no part in making camps, nor in breaking them up. It was women's work.

but scarcely had I stood up when I was overcome with weakness. Raymond had brought up my horse and his mule. I could not even lift the saddle to my horse's back. Raymond saddled her, and I mounted with painful effort. I rode ahead of the Indians, hardly noticing how far ahead I had gone. Then, seeing a storm coming, I turned to see the Indians setting up camp. I was caught by the storm, and fearing the effect the rain might have on me, thought I might die on the prairie.

But the rainstorm was quick and sudden and did not worsen my condition as I had feared. When I arrived back at camp, I borrowed some clothes from Reynal and went back to Big Crow's lodge.

This camp, near the Black Hills, was decided on as the place to leave all the dried meat and unnecessary things. In this way the Indians would be able to move more rapidly toward their proposed hunting grounds. Some even left their lodges there, carrying a few hides with them as shelter from the rain. The food was left up trees to be safe from wolves and grizzly bears. Some set off that afternoon to scout ahead, and in the morning we all set off. Several young men went on ahead as scouts, and we saw them occasionally on the tops of hills, shaking their robes as a signal that they could see buffalo. Soon after, we saw some bulls, and horsemen darted away in pursuit. Then Raymond exclaimed, "Look, Panther is running an antelope!" Panther, on his black and white horse, came at full speed over the hill in hot pursuit of an antelope that darted away like lightning before him. Other Indians cheered, yelled encouragement, and tried to block the flight of the antelope so that Panther might catch up. Yet this was just bravado, for the antelope was bound to outstrip any horse, even that of Panther, for all his skill in riding and hunting.

BRAVERY

Native American ideas about bravery meant that young men were always testing themselves to get a reputation for bravery. Besides counting coup in battle, the warriors used to race their horses, or try to do impossible things. Panther was not trying to catch the antelope; he was trying to see how close he could get to it, showing how fast and gracefully he and his horse could go without stumbling on the uneven ground.

CHAPTER 6

Hail Storm's Buffalo

Later we were to see some more serious sport. A shaggy bull buffalo bounded out from a nearby hollow, and close behind, a Native American boy, riding without stirrups or a saddle. The boy (it was our friend Hail Storm) closed in on the buffalo and let fly three swift arrows into the buffalo. The buffalo tried to catch the pony on his horns, but pony and boy were too quick for him. In a moment they were alongside the buffalo again, which was now driven to desperation. His eyeballs glared through his tangled mane, and blood flew from his mouth and nostrils. That is how they disappeared over the hill.

BUFFALO

Bull buffalo are about 5 feet high at the shoulder. They weigh more than 1 ton. Cow buffalo are smaller, but their hides are more supple and were used to make the lodges. Indians hunted the buffalo down wind, so that their scent was blown away from the buffalo as they approached.

Many Indians rode full speed after them. When we arrived, the buffalo was dead, and the Indians were gathered around him, knives already at work. They knew their work so well that the twisted sinews and bones fell apart as if by magic, and in a moment the vast carcass was reduced to a heap of bloody ruins. The surrounding group of Indians offered no very attractive spectacle to civilized eyes. Some were cracking the huge thigh bones and devouring the **marrow** within; others were cutting away pieces of liver, and other approved morsels, and were swallowing them on the spot with the appetite of wolves. The faces of most of them, besmeared with blood from ear to ear, looked very grim and horrible. My friend White Shield offered me a marrow bone, while another offered me some of the stomach lining. I refused as politely as

I could. Only certain parts of the animal, which would first decay, are eaten on the spot in this way.

We camped for the night, and the next day marched on westward, and kept moving all through the next day. The Indians do not usually spend so much of each day on the move, but they were anxious to reach the hunting ground, kill the necessary number of buffalo, and return from the dangerous neighborhood as soon as possible. We reached a stream they could not name, for they are poorly acquainted with these parts, and had to move farther upstream to camp, and to find enough grass for the horses. We found a meadow to camp in, but when I said to Reynal it was a good camping ground, he replied it was a good place for the Snake to attack us, if they knew we were nearby. The Indians also seemed anxious; they sent out many of the young warriors as scouts. Camp was not finally made until dusk. Mene-Seela and the old men sat down to smoke and talk, and he picked up one of those enormous black and green crickets, which they name "he who points out the buffalo." This creature he respectfully asked where to find the buffalo, and the cricket seemed to point his horns westward. Suddenly a cry went up, and all ran to the gap in the hills that led westward. I could see dark shapes moving there, and was told that these were bands of buffalo cows. The hunting ground was reached at last.

CHAPTER 7

Hunting the Buffalo

Long before daybreak the Indians broke camp to find a better and safer position. Mene-Seela's lodge was the first that was ready for departure. I found the old man himself sitting by the embers of his decaying fire. The Indians were still nervous, and Mene-Seela was impatient with the time it took to dismantle the camp. Eventually he made a speech to the whole village from the center of the circle. Now, he said, when they were on the enemy's hunting grounds, was not the time to behave like children. They should be more active and united than ever. Everyone hurried to help the **laggards**, and we were soon ready to move. We moved some three or four miles upstream, and then the women set up the great ring of the village again.

The warriors did not dismount but, riding their worst horse and leading their best, began to ride away westward over the plains in small groups. I had not eaten, so hurried to Big Crow's lodge and sat down in the middle to show that I was hungry. The squaws soon set a wooden bowl of meat before me, and when I had eaten some, I took a handful of the dried meat the Dakota call **wasna**

WASNA

Wasna was buffalo meat that had been dried in thin strips as soon as it was butchered. The meat kept for longer this way, and was lighter and more easily transported. It was, however, very tough and had to be soaked for a long while before cooking. It was only eaten as dried strips when there was no time to stop to prepare a meal.

which the northern voyagers called **pemmican**) and set off after the
rest of the hunting bands. Soon we were all united into one large and
compact group. We rode at a swift, steady canter, uphill or downhill,
through grass or sagebrush. For an hour and a half, the same brown
shoulders and the same long black hair rose and fell in front of me.
Very little was said, although I thought I saw Raymond being
reproved for leaving his rifle back at the camp.

Several scouts had gone on ahead, and at last we could see several of
them signaling to us at once. The excited Indians now urged forward
their tired horses even more. Reynal and a group of hunters went off
after a small band of buffalo, but Raymond and I stuck with the main
body. Reynal was angered by this, for he had hoped for Raymond's
help in skinning and cutting up any beast that they killed. When they
reached the hill where the scouts were standing, each Indian sprang
from the tired animal he had ridden and mounted the fresher horse he
had led.

A surround, painted by George Catlin, 1832–1833. The first few minutes of a buffalo hunt were usually chaotic, as the Indians needed to split the big herds up into smaller groups so that they could be more easily killed. This picture conveys the confusion, but cannot really give an idea of the noise or the dustiness — if the artist had shown the dust, we would be unable to see anything else.

This picture by Eagle Lance, a Dakota who drew a picture history of his people in the late nineteenth century, shows buffalo being skinned and cut up. This first butchering was done by the women and children, and then the meat and hides were taken back to camp for cleaning, drying, and treating.

There were no saddles nor bridles in the whole party. A piece of buffalo hide served in place of a saddle, and a cord of twisted buffalo hair served as a guiding rein. Eagle feathers dangled from manes and tails, as signs of courage and speed. The Indians wore nothing but a sort of kilt and moccasins. They had heavy whips made of elk horn and hide. They held their bows in their hands, and their arrows were held in quivers of otter or panther skin, slung over their shoulders.

From the next hill we sighted a herd of some 500 cow buffalo, crowded together by the banks of a wide stream that was soaking across the sand beds of the valley. They were guarded by some old bull buffalo, but these fled as soon as they scented our approach, attacking only if their escape was blocked. Each hunter, as if by common impulse, struck his horse, each horse sprang forward, and scattering in our charge to assault the entire herd at once, we rushed at the buffalo. We were on them in an instant. Amid the trampling and the yells, I could see dark figures running hither and thither in the dust, with horsemen in pursuit. The uproar and confusion lasted but a moment. When the dust cleared, the herd of buffalo could be seen scattered on the plain, fleeing either singly or in groups, pursued by Indians riding at a furious speed, yelling as they launched arrow after arrow into their sides. There were already many carcasses on the plain, and wounded, dying buffalo, their sides feathered with arrows, which

CLOTHES

Native American clothing varied according to the seasons. When Parkman was with the Indians, it was summer, so they wore very little. In the winter they would have worn trousers and a tunic made from buffalo hide, painted and decorated with beads and feathers (see p.43).

USES OF THE BUFFALO

Hides: lodges, clothing, containers, ropes, shields. Used with the fur on as sleeping blankets and clothes

Horns: cups, ladles, toys, headdresses

Bones: knives, tools, arrowheads, needles, dice

Hooves: glue, tools, babies' rattles

Sinews: bowstring, thread

Brains: making the hides soft to tan them

Fat: cooking, soap

Dung: dried, as fuel

Tail: fly swats and ornaments

Head: skull often used in religious ceremonies

Hair: rope, string, stuffing for pillows

Tongue: food, hairbrushes

Meat: food, some dried in strips

would try to gore my horse if I passed too close.

Raymond and I crossed the plain together, counting up scores of buffalo carcasses, while far away in the distance horsemen and buffalo were still charging along, with clouds of dust rising behind them. The boys who had been waiting behind the brow of the hill holding the horses appeared and began the work of skinning and cutting up in earnest. I noticed Big Crow just dismounting by the side of a bull that he had killed. The arrow was entirely buried in the body of the animal, but for the feathered notch at the end.

The hides and meat were piled onto the horses, and the hunters began to leave the ground. I asked Raymond to guide me back to the village. Big Crow's squaw brought me food and water and a buffalo robe, and I fell instantly asleep. I awoke when Big Crow returned, his arms smeared to the elbows in blood. His squaw gave him water to wash in and meat to eat. Then she took off his bloody moccasins and put fresh ones on his feet. He fell asleep. Now the hunters were returning, and vast piles of meat and hides were gathered in front of every lodge. Darkness fell, and fires were lit. The squaws and children searched the piles of meat for the daintiest portions. They ate some raw and set others to roast on the fire. The hunters woke and grouped around the fire, eating and telling stories of bravery seen and done during the day's hunting.

Chapter 8

Daily Life

We stayed camped on this spot for five days, and for the first three the hunters were incessantly at work. There was much alarm about staying so long in enemy territory, and everyone was alert. To make the enemy think that we had greater numbers, there were sticks and stones piled on the top of nearby hills to give the impression that we had sentinels constantly on the watch. It was a scene to remember, the tall white rocks, the old pine trees, the sandy stream that ran below the hills and half enclosed the village, and the wild sage bushes, which gave off such a distinctive odor.

Hour after hour the squaws passed and repassed with their vessels of water between the stream and the lodges. While the men were hunting, we saw only the women and children, a few old men, and even fewer lazy ones. Yet it was still a busy and bustling scene. In all quarters the meat was hung on cords of hide to dry in the sun. Around the lodges

Sioux village life, painted by George Catlin in 1830. Buffalo skins were cleaned, and the meat was dried in the sun in strips to make wasna.

he squaws, young and old, were laboring on the fresh hides, which hey stretched on the ground, scraping the hair from one side and the lesh from the other, and rubbing buffalo brains onto them to make hem soft and pliant.

The fourth day it was still quiet in the village, though the hunters had not gone out that day and lay sleeping in their lodges. Most of the women were silently going about their heavy tasks and working on the buffalo that remained to be treated. One of the tasks was a general division of the meat, for while the tongue and the hide of the buffalo belonged to the hunter who killed it, the rest of the carcass was looked on as belonging to the whole village. So the weak, the old, and even the lazy came in for a share of the spoils. In this way many a helpless old woman, who would otherwise have starved, was kept in plenty.

A squaw from the next lodge, an excellent housekeeper called Good Woman, brought us a large bowl of wasna, and squealed with delight when I presented her with a green glass ring, one of a number I kept about me for these occasions. By now it was nearly dark; fires were lit and kettles were filled with meat and surrounded by women and children who chattered merrily.

A circle of a different kind formed in the center of the village, made up of the old men and warriors of great repute, who sat with their white buffalo robes drawn around their shoulders, passing the pipe around from hand to hand and telling stories. I sat with them, and even took my part in the storytelling. I then played a trick on them by setting off some **squibs** made from gunpowder that I had made one day by the creek. I lit them and tossed them into the air, and they whizzed and spluttered away over the heads of the company. The Indians all ran off with yelps of astonishment and consternation. Then, one by one, they ventured back, the boldest of them picking up the burnt cases and working out their "magic." This is just the sort of joke that the Indian likes, and so I got myself a good reputation by it.

When I reached Big Crow's lodge, I saw, by the blaze of the fire in the middle, that he was asleep in his usual place. His couch consisted of buffalo robes laid together on the ground and a pillow made of whitened deer skin, stuffed with feathers, and ornamented with beads. At his back there was a light framework of poles and reeds, on which he could lean with ease when in a sitting posture. His bow and his quiver were hung at the top of the framework. His squaw, a laughing broad-faced woman, was still bustling about the lodge, organizing his cases of dried meat and various utensils. There were also some half a dozen children scattered about, sleeping anywhere they wanted. My saddle was in its place at the head of the lodge, where guests are supposed to sleep and sit, with a buffalo robe beside it. I wrapped myself up and lay down, hoping to be able to sleep.

It was hard to sleep in the village. This night was harder because of the noise in the next lodge. Some twenty voices were chanting in time to the heavy, monotonous beat of a drum. The Indians there were gambling, the players staking their ornaments, their horses, and even as the excitement rose their weapons. I fell asleep with the dull drum notes in my ear; the gambling went on until daybreak.

I was wakened in the night by one of the children crawling over me, but I repelled these advances with a short stick that I always had with me for this purpose. Sleeping half the day and eating too much makes the children restless; I often had to beat them off four or five times in a night. My host, Big Crow, also disturbed my sleep. All Indians see themselves as bound to perform certain acts to be sure of success in

A decorated buffalo robe. Designs on these robes could show scenes from the life of its owner, scenes from a well-known story, or have a decorative pattern.

A gambling bowl, with counters and tally sticks. The men would bet a number of tally sticks on how the counters would fall when they landed in the bowl.

A Sioux medicine man's bag and its contents. There is a rattle to frighten away evil spirits, two tortoise shells to use as drinking cups and to mix potions, and many bags of herbs and roots. This medicine bag had over twenty different small bags of powders in it.

war, love, or any other part of life. These so called "medicines" come to them in dreams. So one Indian might always strike his pipe on the ground before lighting it, and another may feel that he has to drink a bowl of water immediately upon sighting a white man. My host had been told by his spirits to sing a certain song in the middle of every night; regularly at about twelve o'clock, I would be roused by his chanting. The dogs would then see fit to wake and howl altogether at about two or three in the morning, a noise that is bad enough heard at a distance, on the prairie, let alone when you are sleeping in its midst.

I wish now to consider Big Crow as a father and a husband. Both he and his squaw, like most Indians, were very fond of their children, whom they indulged to excess and never punished except in extreme cases, when they would throw a bowl of cold water over them. Their children became wild, disrespectful, and disobedient under this system, which tended to foster the idea that there was no need for restraint, something that lies at the heart of the Indian character. He was less tender as a husband. His squaw had been with him for many years and took sole care of his children and his household concerns. They did not quarrel, but his affections were reserved for another squaw, who lived in a lodge some distance from his. Yet one day this one displeased him for some reason, and he pushed her out of the lodge, with all her clothes and ornaments, and told her to return to her father. This done he returned to his own lodge and smoked a pipe in tranquillity.

There were many tales of war told by the fire, which showed that the Indians were both brave and cruel. Once captured, enemies were often subjected to the cruelest of tortures; their bodies were often terribly scarred, and Big Crow told a story of one war party roasting an enemy alive. Yet it was not just their enemies they marked like this. When I asked Big Crow about his scars, I found that some of them were self-inflicted during ceremonies to appease the spirits.

You will remember that my original aim was to see something of Native American warfare, and that there had been talk of the village going to war after the hunt. This idea had been largely forgotten, except by a party of eleven warriors who wanted to fight the Snake Indians. The party's leader was a warrior called White Shield, whom I had often visited in his lodge.

Just as all seemed set for war, White Shield was taken ill with an inflammation of the throat and much shivering. He came to Reynal, hoping he or I might have medicine that would help, but finding we had none, he went to one of the medicine men of the village. This old imposter thumped White Shield for some time with his fists, howled and yelled over him, and beat a drum by his ear to drive out the evil spirit that he said was lodged there. This failed to have any effect, and White Shield returned to his lodge, certain he was possessed of an evil spirit. But that afternoon he announced that the Snake had killed his brother, and that he and the other warriors would go to fight them the next day, for the death had gone unpunished for too long. Yet when he said this, he looked dejected and listless, not his usual brave self. That evening he dressed in his war clothes and painted his face and his horse, and rode around the village singing his war song.

The next morning I was up eager to see their departure, but nothing happened. At last White Shield came to see Reynal and myself, and Reynal asked why the party had not set out. White Shield made excuses about not having enough arrows, and then said that one of his warriors had had a dream that the spirits of the dead were throwing stones at the war party, and said this meant they should not go. Had this dream really happened it would have been an excellent reason not to go, but Reynal was certain that the dream was an excuse, and that White Shield did not have the heart to go. This is one of the strange things about the Indian; he is brave and fierce in battle, yet if he feels that spirits are against him, or that he is possessed of a bad spirit, he seems to lose all his will.

All idea of war was abandoned, and it was decided to return to the part of the plains that the village regarded as their territory. On June 25, late in the afternoon, we broke camp, with the usual tumult and

CHAPTER 9

War at Last

DREAMS

Indians saw dreams as belonging to two groups. There were ordinary dreams, which often were unremarkable and only half-remembered. These were not seen as important. Other dreams were sent by animal spirits or ghosts of ancestors and were seen as very significant. Once the meanings of the dreams were worked out, Indians had to obey them, even if they did not want to.

Right
A medicine man, one of the Hidatsa tribe, in the costume of the Dog Dance painted by Karl Bodmer. The Dog Dancers were a religious society, like the Arrow Breakers. Each society had members in different villages, and each had their own dances and songs, which had to be sung at certain times and places.

confusion. We all moved forward across the plains, but we only managed to advance a few miles. I was in Big Crow's lodge, just in the act of taking off my powder horn and bullet pouch when, close at hand, loud, shrill, and in good earnest, came the terrific yell of a war whoop. Big Crow's squaw snatched up the youngest child and fled from the lodge, the other children following.

I followed and found the village in utter confusion. The old men had gone from the center, warriors were darting about, weapons in hand, and running with wild yells to the far end of the village. Reynal was calling from the far side of the stream, and I could see Raymond going toward him. It was certainly going to be the safest place to be unless we wished to involve ourselves in the fray. The women were screaming and looking for places of safety, their children in their arms. On rising ground near the camp were a line of old women, singing a medicine song to allay the tumult. It was at this point that I realized that we were not under attack, for the crowd had separated into two long lines of warriors, confronting each other at a respectful distance, jumping about and dodging one another's bullets and arrows. Yet, as the sharp humming sounds [of arrows] close to my head bore out, the danger was no less real for being internal. I quickly forded the brook and sat with Reynal and Raymond to watch the result.

The disturbance, amazingly, was over almost as soon as it began. The separate lines became a mass once more, and although there was yelling, there was no more firing. Five or six people bustled about as if acting as peacemakers. At last the crowd began to disperse, and in a quarter of an hour, all was quiet. There was a circle in the center of the village again, although I did not join them, for the pipe was moving from left to right, contrary to the usual order, a sign that it was a "medicine-pipe" of conciliation, when I would not be welcome.

It was not until later that I found out the cause of the disturbance. The Dakota have several fraternal groups, which have social, warlike, and magical links. One of these was the Arrow Breakers, of which four lived in our village, and who were distinguished by their hair, which bristled high above their heads, adding to their height and giving them a ferocious appearance. One of these was Mad Wolf, whom I had always thought to be the most dangerous man in the village. Mad Wolf wanted a horse belonging to Tall Bear. He had given Tall Bear a gift of a horse of nearly the same value, knowing that Tall Bear, by custom, would have to give the horse Mad Wolf desired in return. Tall Bear did not immediately return the gift, as would be the custom. Mad Wolf, growing impatient, openly took the horse, at which Tall Bear flew into a rage, took out his knife, and severely wounded the horse. From this all the rest had come.

CHAPTER 10

The Black Hills

We traveled east for two days; then the gloomy ridges of the Black Hills rose up before us. The village followed the line of the hills for some time, and then entered a pass into the mountains, which had a stream running through it that was dotted with beaver lodges and dams. The pass got narrower; then it suddenly opened out into a broad, grassy meadow, where we stopped, and the camp rose as if by magic.

The lodges were hardly pitched when the Indians set about accomplishing the purpose that had brought them here—obtaining poles for their new lodges. About half the company, men, women and boys, mounted horses and set off deep into the mountains. They climbed at full gallop over the shingly rocks, passing with apparent ease beside steep precipices. Sometimes we followed a course among the trees, sometimes they would gallop wildly past me on the open spaces, the men whooping, laughing, and lashing their horses. After some eight miles, we came upon a forest of spruce trees.

The Indians immediately spread out and began to cut poles for themselves with their hatchets and knives. Raymond went to help Reynal, and I was left alone; yet the sounds of the hatchets and of voices could be heard all around. I climbed farther up the mountain, and was full of admiration for the wild beauty of the place. At last I

This Sun Dance ceremony was painted by George Catlin in 1837. The Indians believed that by resisting pain they were completing a kind of test that would show how brave they were and win them approval. In the Sun Dance, the warriors who took part had their chests pierced in two places so that a piece of hide could be passed through the hole and tied. The other end of the hide was tied to the central pole. The warriors then danced around the pole until the hide either broke or tore away their skin, or until they passed out.

ade my way back to camp. The camp was full of newly cut poles; ome were already prepared and lay white and glistening, drying the sun. The squaws, boys, and even some of the warriors were vorking on others, peeling off the bark and shaping them. Most of e hides from the buffalo we had caught were now **supple** enough be worked, and the squaws were busy sewing them together with **inew**.

fter breakfast the next day, Reynal, Raymond, and I went hunting the mountains. We failed to catch anything, and I severely cracked ny rifle in a fall. Our annoyance was increased to meet Hailstorm ith the carcass of a female elk, which he had caught in the same nountains just a mile from camp. In the morning I found, to my reat disgust, that we were to stay there another day, so I went unting alone. I came upon Mene-Seela, seated alone, as unmoving s a statue. His eyes were fixed on the gently swaying top of a pine ree. He was obviously engaged in some religious ritual, for the ndian sees all of nature as having a mystic influence; he watches the ature around him as an astrologer watches the stars. So closely is he inked with it that his guardian spirit is often the form of a living reature, or even a living thing, such as a pine tree. I did not disturb im, but crept away back into the mountains.

THE GREAT SPIRIT

The Native Americans believed in Waken Tanka, the Great Spirit, who created the world and made everything on the earth dependent on everything else. The Indians believed that people, animals, and the earth itself should help one another. This was why they never hunted more animals than they needed, and why they expected animals to help them, if they asked in the right way. The rituals they performed were all based on this belief that there was a right way to ask Waken Tanka, and as a result help would be given somehow.

CHAPTER 11

Farewells

Back at the camp I found that the Indians had decided to return in the direction of Fort Laramie, which I should have to do also to keep my rendezvous with Shaw. First we had to move some two miles south to find a pass through the mountains. I rode some way with Panther, who used this name to disguise his real name, which like many Indians he concealed out of superstition. He was a noble-looking fellow, clad in his decorated buffalo robe, with the long feathers of the prairie cock fluttering on the crown of his head. He was a very sympathetic-looking fellow, and did not seem to have the suspicious and treacherous nature of many Indians. As we rode along, he taught me many words in the Dakota language.

The crossing of the mountains was done without alarms, and that evening when we were some two days from the fort, I sat down to smoke what I thought would be a farewell pipe with my newfound friends. I had decided to set out in advance of them, and hurry as fast as I could to reach Fort Laramie, for it was already August 1, the day that Shaw and I had agreed to meet. I went to see Hail Storm and offered the remains of my trinkets if he would guide me with all speed toward the fort the next day. He agreed, and I went back to Big Crow's lodge. Long before daylight I was wakened by Raymond and went out into the chill damp morning. Despite rising so early, it was not possible to get far in advance of the village, and we spent much of the day within sight and sound of them, even having taken our leave. We ended up spending another night in their company. The heat in the camp that night was intense, and the coverings of the lodges were raised some foot or more from the ground to provide some circulation. Once again I smoked a farewell pipe with a circle of Indian friends.

In the morning Reynal directed us to a landmark that would lead us to the fort. We said our goodbyes to Reynal, but not to the Indians, as they do not hold with formal leave taking at the time of departure. After a day and a night on the plain, we sighted the fort from the summit of a sandy hill. It lay some miles below us, standing by the side of the river like a little gray speck. I stopped my horse and sat for a moment looking down on it. It suddenly seemed to me to be the center of comfort and civilization. We rode to it at great speed, and arrived to find Shaw and his guides waiting for us at the gate, having seen us coming from some way off.

GUIDES

It is interesting that it was only during the last few days of his stay in the Indian village that Parkman mentions learning any of the Dakota language. Most whites who visited the Indians in this way did not bother with the language. They relied mostly on their guides to translate their words for them, and got by the rest of the time with gestures and signs.

A Sioux warrior, painted by Karl Bodmer in 1833. Warriors were proud of their appearance. Many of the things they wore showed how brave they were as warriors — like the eagle feathers in their hair.

CHAPTER 12

Going Home

I was delighted to see my friend again, as he was to see me, having feared that some disaster might have befallen me. We ate and slept, and the next day was spent with Shaw telling me of his adventures, and of what had been going on in the fort in my absence. On August 4, early in the afternoon, we left Fort Laramie and turned our horses' heads for home. For some while we had trappers for company, as well as our guides, and we spent some days with them at the Indian village where they lived. One evening a horse racing contest was held on the prairie, for which Indians came from a long way away to compete. Their skill and speed in horse racing was a wonder to see. The swiftest were given eagle feathers to put in their horses' manes and tails.

We then continued on our way, following the course of the Platte River, then crossed the ridge that separates that river from the Arkansas. Finally we arrived at the fort called the Pueblo, a dilapidated square mud enclosure peopled by Mexicans with their squaws and Spanish women. A trader told us that there was much unrest in the area, and that we might need to stay some while for safety. But we decided to push on as fast as we could and reached Bent's Fort without incident.

INDIAN UNREST

Parkman was on the Plains at a time when the Indians were coming more into contact with the whites, and were having their first problems with white soldiers. Parkman was puzzled by the growing hostility, and by the lack of warmth of other Indians such as the Arapaho. He was lucky to have traveled when he did; the idea that traveling among the Indians was a gentleman's pastime, and a warm welcome could be expected as a right, was soon to break down completely, as the trust between the Indians and the whites dissolved in the face of white greed.

Once again we were warned of unrest; but we decided to continue and followed the banks of the Arkansas, meeting parties of settlers, traders, **Mormons**, and even some Arapaho Indians. These Indians let us visit their village and took presents from us. They did not attack us, but neither did they smoke with us, and our visit to their village was full of unease. Still we were allowed to go on our way and had a chance to hunt some buffalo as we went, enough to provide us with meat to cross the frontier.

At last we passed through the land of the no-longer-nomadic Shawanoes, who have settled and farm the land. Then Westport was before us, and we made our way to Kansas Landing, where we had disembarked from the steamboat so long before. Deslauriers came the next day, looking strange with a shaven face, hat, and coat, offering to give a feast on our account that night. But the arrival of the steamboat prevented us from attending the festivities. Deslauriers waved us off, and we were gone. There followed eight days of travel to St. Louis (about a third of that time being spent on sandbars), and then a fortnight of railroads, coaches, and steamboats before we saw the familiar features of home.

Horse racing near Fort Clark, painted in 1833. Horse races were important training for the Indians in preparation for a lifetime of hunting.

Glossary

animal spirit the form of a particular animal or bird, which is supposed to have magical powers.

appointments equipment

buffalo robes skins made from the hide of buffalo, used as blankets and as a sort of cloak.

civilization when referred to by Parkman, the ways of the whites.

counting coup touching an enemy or his horse in battle, rather than killing him.

Dakota *see tribes.*

Delawares *see tribes.*

democratic making decisions by consulting people.

dignitaries important people.

emigrants people who move to live in another country, or in the case of America, another part of the same continent.

Foxes *see tribes.*

freight cargo, things being transported.

futility uselessness.

Great Spirit *see Waken Tanka.*

homeopathy the treatment of a disease by giving a drug in small doses that would, in a healthy person, produce symptoms like those of the disease.

imposter someone who pretends to be someone else.

inflammation when a wound or a part of the body become red, swollen, and sore.

Kansas *see tribes.*

kettle a pot on the fire.

laggard someone who lingers, always behind.

lance a sort of spear.

lodge *either* the tent home of a Native American family *or* a group of men who come together to perform particular magic ceremonies.

mallet a wooden hammer, usually with a handle in the middle.

marrow a soft edible mixture that is in the middle of big bones.

moccasins Indian shoes, made from buffalo hides.

Mormon a member of a religious group founded in America in 1830.

mountain men trappers and hunters who lived in the wild.

Negro term used until the mid-twentieth century to refer to African Americans.

officials men in the Indian village respected for their fair-mindedness, who were expected to help to sort out quarrels.

pemmican *see wasna.*

picket to tether a horse to a piece of wood fixed in the ground.

prairies the flat lands of the great plains.

primeval Parkman means primitive.

quiver case often made of buffalo hide, for holding arrows.

Sacs *see tribes.*

Shawanoes *see tribes.*

sinew the strong cord that connects muscle with bone, used for binding, tying, and as thread.

squaw an Indian woman or wife.

squib a type of firework that usually explodes when lit.

steamboat riverboats that went up the Missouri, which were moved by two paddlewheels on either side of the boat.

supple capable of bending without breaking or cracking.

surround a way of catching buffalo, by surrounding them.

travois the sledge that Indians hitched to dogs or horses to pull their possessions.

tribes different groups of Native Americans. Each tribe was split into many villages. Parkman was visiting one village of the Oglala people, a group that was part of the Sioux tribe (who called themselves the Dakota). The tribes had different languages and customs, and lived in different areas. Tribes often fought each other. The various tribes that Parkman saw in Westport (Sacs, Foxes, Shawanoes, Delawares, Kansas, and Wyandots) were Indians who had already been made to share their land with the whites, and who lived with them, rather than living separate lives like the Sioux Parkman was going to visit.

trinkets cheap gifts such as rings, necklaces, and beads.

vagrant wandering, traveling, with no fixed home.

vermilion a red plant dye.

Waken Tanka the Great Spirit, who the Indians believed created everything.

Wasna dried strips of buffalo meat.

Wyandots *see tribes.*

Index

Numbers in *italic* type refer to captions; numbers in **bold** type refer to information boxes.

© Heinemann Educational 1993